sundance
publishing

LITTLE RED
READERS

The Scarecrow

**PETER SLOAN &
SHERYL SLOAN**

Illustrated by Virginia Barrett

A farmer made a scarecrow.

Along came a horse.

The scarecrow scared the horse.
The horse ran away.

Along came a dog.

The scarecrow scared the dog.
The dog ran away.

Along came a cow.

The scarecrow scared the cow.
The cow ran away.

Along came a pig.

The scarecrow scared the pig.
The pig ran away.

Along came a goat.

The scarecrow scared the goat.
The goat ran away.

Along came a crow.

The scarecrow <u>did not</u> scare the crow.
The crow stayed.

Along came a cat.

The cat scared the crow.
The crow flew away.